PRESENTS

THE DEFINITIVE GUIDE TO
MINECRAFT
2025

A TOTALLY INDEPENDENT PUBLICATION

ISBN 978-1-915994-42-4

PILLAR
BOX
RED

Written by Naomi Berry
Designed by Adam Wilsher

WELCOME

Welcome, fellow adventurers!

Whether you're a seasoned miner or just embarking on your very first quest, this book is ready to be your ultimate companion to all things Minecraft, packed with tips, tricks and challenges to take your skills to the next level (be it subterranean or even trans-dimensional).

From crafting epic gear to combat tips to have you fighting like a pro, we've got you covered. But all work and no play is a dull ride, so we're sure to make it a fun one with brain-bending puzzles and quizzes to test your Minecraft mastery.

So grab your trusty pickaxe and prepare for an epic trip through the pixelated landscapes of Minecraft. Building towering fortresses? Battling undead pig zombies? Burning down innocent villages? Baking the perfect birthday cake?

Whatever your fancy, let's begin.

Happy mining!

CONTENTS

GLOSSARY

The world of Minecraft is as complex as it is vast, with a whole dictionary of in-game terms that could make even the most seasoned of Minecraft miners stutter a little, never mind a newbie.

So before you go spelunking in any caves, plundering any villages or questing for a forbidden portal to transport you to a hellscape, why not brush up on your Minecraft-ese?

ADVENTURE

The Adventure game mode is all about player-created maps, with more specific gameplay goals in mind rather than just survival.

ALEX

Alex is the female default skin for the player character.

AFK

This acronym isn't Minecraft specific per se, but more gaming in general. It stands for 'away from keyboard'.

BEDROCK

The foundational block of the Minecraft world. If you're digging downwards and you hit bedrock, that's as far as you're going, bud.

BIOME

The Minecraft map is made up of varying geographical regions called biomes. Each biome has its own distinct weather, vegetation and mobs.

There's way more to know about biomes, so much so that we can't fit it all in a mere glossary entry. Check out the Biomes 101 chapter (p. 14-17) to learn more about all of the biomes you can find in the game.

BLOCK

Every single thing in Minecraft is made up entirely of blocks. These little pixelated cubes are the very foundation that the Minecraft world is built on.

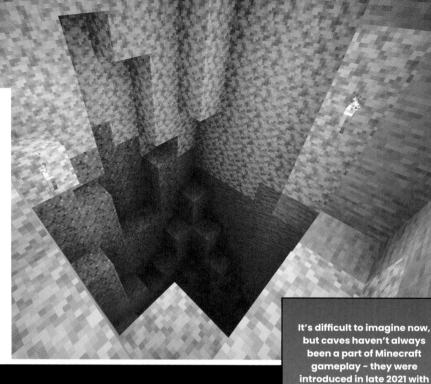

CAVING

The world of Minecraft is rich with resources, but if you're diving down into a cave to find some, then you're caving, to be precise. Caving can be a whole sub-game of its own, since so many are part of a huge honeycomb of underground chambers and habitats.

It's difficult to imagine now, but caves haven't always been a part of Minecraft gameplay - they were introduced in late 2021 with the Caves & Cliffs update, one of the most significant updates the game had seen since its release.

CHUNK

A 16x16 area (from sky to bedrock) used as a measurement to render distance in Minecraft.

COORDS

Shorthand for coordinates, these are used to note a specific position in the Minecraft world.

CRAFT

It's impossible to succeed in Minecraft without utilising the Crafting mechanic, which allows you to take resources from the world around you and use them to create different items. You can learn more about Crafting on p. 46.

CREATIVE

Creative Mode eliminates all survival aspects of Minecraft gameplay and lets players really flex their creative prowess with an endless supply of blocks to create with.

Creative
Build and explore without limits. You can fly, have endless materials and can't be hurt by monsters.

CRIT

Crit is shorthand for critical hit. Crits deal x1.5 damage instead of the x.1, and can be triggered when striking a target on the downward trajectory of a jump. Successful crits are signalled by a brown X on the target.

DROP

After destroying a block or defeating a mob, there's a good chance it will leave something behind. This little present is a drop.

ELYTRA

An Elytra is a legendary glider that can be used to fly across the map. In Survival mode, it's super rare and can only be found in End Ships.

ENCHANT

Enchanting is a gameplay mechanic that allows you to upgrade your gear. Unlike Crafting (which you'll be using from your first day to your last), this mechanic only becomes of real significant use in late-game survival runs.

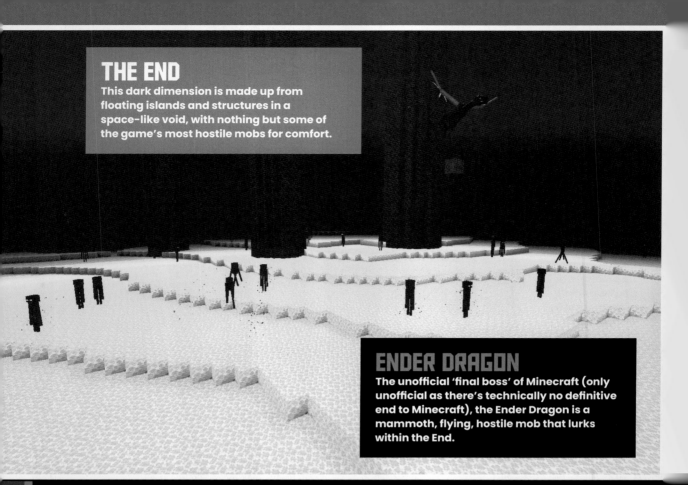

THE END

This dark dimension is made up from floating islands and structures in a space-like void, with nothing but some of the game's most hostile mobs for comfort.

ENDER DRAGON

The unofficial 'final boss' of Minecraft (only unofficial as there's technically no definitive end to Minecraft), the Ender Dragon is a mammoth, flying, hostile mob that lurks within the End.

FIRE RES

Short for fire resistance, this potion makes the player immune to fire and lava.

HARDCORE

Survival mode with the difficulty jacked up to 100. This mode is exclusive to the Java edition, and is only for those looking for a real challenge. There's no second chances, either - if you die, the whole world goes with you.

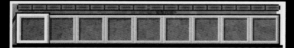

HOTBAR

The first nine slots in your inventory, a kind of shortlist of your most useful and used items.

HOTKEY

Switching between items in your hotbar with speed. It's a little finickity to get down, but once you know your hotbar layout well, it'll be like muscle memory.

INVIS

Short for invisibility potion, which (surprise, surprise) makes you invisible to mobs or other players.

MLG

This acronym stands for 'major league gaming', and is basically used whenever a player does anything particularly impressive to avoid taking damage. Throwing a water bucket underneath you right before impact from a fall? MLG. Block clutching? MLG. You get the gist.

MOB

The creatures of Minecraft are referred to as mobs, friendly and hostile alike. Knowing your mobs is a key part of surviving in any Minecraft dimension, so make sure to brush up on the mobs on p. 28-31.

MOD

Minecraft mods ("modifications") are user-created and are created to change the game's base content. You can download and install mods, but always be careful when deciding what to add to your game; not all mods are made equal, and some can affect how well the game runs.

MOJANG

Where would we be without Mojang? In a world without Minecraft – that's where! Mojang Studios are the developers behind this very game.

MOJANG
STUDIOS

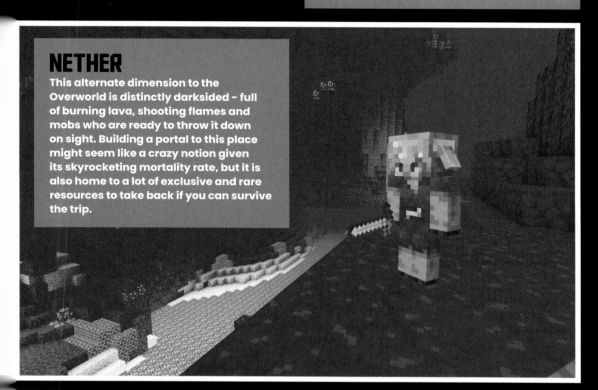

NETHER

This alternate dimension to the Overworld is distinctly darksided – full of burning lava, shooting flames and mobs who are ready to throw it down on sight. Building a portal to this place might seem like a crazy notion given its skyrocketing mortality rate, but it is also home to a lot of exclusive and rare resources to take back if you can survive the trip.

OVERWORLD

It's likely you'll spend most of your term travelling across the vast expanse that is the Overworld: the main world of Minecraft. It may not be as openly hostile as the other dimensions, but be wary when travelling across certain biomes – they're not all friendly ground.

PICKAXE

A very trusty and necessary tool used to mine ores and rocks throughout all three dimensions. Different types of pickaxes have different efficiencies, depending on what material they're crafted from.

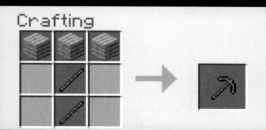

PORTAL

The only method of travel between the three dimensions. Nether portals will take you to the Nether, and end portals will take you to the End. In Survival, nether portals usually have to be built from scratch with obsidian, but you might come across the odd incomplete nether portal in the Overworld that requires just one or two extra blocks. End portals are much harder to find - you'll need eyes of ender to locate one in a stronghold portal room, and then nine eyes of ender to fill in the blocks to activate it.

For more information on interdimensional travel, check out The Three Dimensions on p. 12-13!

PROT

Short for protection, which refers to the stat enchantments placed on your armour.

PVE/PVP

Shorthand for Player v. Environment and Player v. Player.

RNG

RNG is short for random number generator, which is the system that determines random qualities of your game. Players generally use it to mean lucky ("good rng") or unlucky ("bad rng").

SANDBOX

Games with open world design allow players the freedom to create, edit and explore the world they find themselves in are referred to as sandbox games. Unlike games with narratives or fixed objectives, sandbox games put the creative control in the hands of the player, and let them craft their own gameplay experience.

SEED

Seeds are randomly generated codes that create all of the different Minecraft worlds - kind of like world templates. Sharing seeds allow players to generate the same kind of world in their own games.

SERVER
An online space where players hang out and play together.

SKELLY

Minecraft-speak for skeleton mobs.

SKIN

Steve and Alex may be the OGs, but you have plenty of other options for dressing your player character. These special costumes come in the form of skins.

SNIPING

Minecraft may not have the arsenal of say, Fortnite, but you can still snipe. In Minecraft, sniping is shooting enemies with an arrow.

SPAWN

Your spawn spot is wherever you first appear in a Minecraft world (coordinate-wise). If you die without setting a respawn point (God forbid), then you'll respawn allllllll the way back where you first dropped into the world. Be smart, kids. Set your respawn points.

Survival
Explore a mysterious world where you build, collect, craft and fight monsters.

SPECTATOR

This game mode lets players fly around the world and, well, spectate. You can't interact with any elements of the world, but it can be useful to scope out worlds. You can even use it to see the world through the eyes of a mob.

SURVIVAL

Survival mode is the quintessential Minecraft experience, where players travel the world, gather resources and there's only one definitive goal: keep surviving. It's all about staying alive for as long as you can, so you have to keep an eye on your health and hunger, set up a shelter and strategize your inventory to stretch out your game as long as you can.

STACK

The longer your game runs, the more things you'll end up collecting. Your inventory can get out of control real quick, so employing stacks is a good way to keep on top of things in larger quantities. Stacking items together (up to 64) into one slot allows you to save inventory space and also know how much you have of a resource at a glance.

VANILLA

When you play Minecraft without any mods or plugins, then you're playing the 'vanilla' version.

Inventory management is no joke! Having a well-organised and strategic inventory can be as important as crafting strong weapons to your chances of survival. Inventory Essentials on p. 44-45 has plenty of tips to getting the most out of your inventory - it's way more than just throwing stuff in chests!

WITHER

If the Ender Dragon is the game's ultimate boss, then the Wither is its deputy in chief. The Wither is a particularly tough boss opponent that can be summoned with soul sand and wither skeleton skulls. Taking it on is not for the weak-hearted, and is best saved for late-game adventures.

STEVE

Mr. Minecraft himself! Steve is the default male skin for the player character, and basically the face of the whole game.

XP

XP (experience points) is the currency needed to enchant and repair items. Players can gain XP through defeating hostile mobs, mining, smelting and cooking, breeding... basically making use of all the gameplay mechanics that Minecraft has to offer.

THE THREE DIMENSIONS

Your journey across the world of Minecraft will see you cross all sorts of environments, discover bustling settlements, abandoned structures and a whole lot of mobs (some of which aren't particularly pleased to be discovered) – oh, and don't forget a casual spot of interdimensional travel. The world of Minecraft is split into three dimensions: the Overworld, the Nether and the End.

THE OVERWORLD

Most players end up spending most of their time up on the Overworld. It's where your adventure begins, when you spawn into the Overworld with naught but your stubby pixel hands and a dream. You can play a very fulfilling and gameplay mechanic-rich game up here without ever having to venture through a portal.

The Overworld is by far the biggest and most diverse of the three realms, with the biggest variety of biomes and mob inhabitants. It's also the only dimension that has a day and night cycle. The cycle affects the environment, such as the sunlight being able to grow plants. The sun always rises in the east and sets in the west, just like it does in our real world.

The Overworld is the tallest of the three realms, with a vertical height of 384 blocks (the other two only clock in at 256).

THE NETHER

This hellscape is a dimension full of bursts of fire, oceans of lava and exploding beds. Yes, exploding beds.

So what's the draw? The Nether may be difficult to traverse, but it's worth it – it's full of special and rare ores and resources that you just can't find up on the Overworld.

If you want to travel to the Nether, you'll need to make (or find) yourself a Nether portal. You can create one with 14 pieces of obsidian (or just 10, if you want to skip out on the corner pieces) in a rectangular frame, then activate it by using some form of fire in the middle.

The usual fire starter is flint and steel, but you can also get a little creative with a fire charge, fireball, lighting strike, or even a well-steered forest fire.

You might not need all 12 eyes of ender – there's a 10% chance that an end portal block comes with an eye of ender already in it.

THE END

If the Nether is a hellscape, then the End is like walking into a nightmare. This barren realm is a void filled with floating end stone islands and structures.

Travelling to the End is the closest to an end game objective as Minecraft has to offer. Players can spend their time in the Overworld and the Nether building up their gear and preparing to head to the End, make it through and take on the Ender Dragon.

If you're ready to take on the challenge, you have to seek out an end portal in a stronghold. Eyes of ender are rare craftable items that can be used to track (and lead you to) the nearest stronghold. Once you find a portal, you need to put 12 eyes of ender into it (one in each block) in order to activate it.

BIOMES 101

Players spend most of their time up in the Overworld, exploring its vast and different landscapes and environments - these are called biomes. Each biome has its own unique look, resources, and even weather conditions.

Arid biomes never experience rain or snowfall

ARID LAND BIOMES

Highlands are biomes that exist way up on the Y-axis. The terrain is typically rugged and sparse in vegetation. These biomes can be grouped into three categories.

Badlands: This is an uncommon biome, identifiable by its red sand and veins of gold. The abandoned mines are worth exploring for treasure, but they're also home to hostile mobs.

Deserts: This is the most common of the arid biomes. The desert is full of sand, sandstone and a cactus or two.

Savannas: This biome is characterised by its flat land and acacia or oak trees. Despite being arid, it's not a bad place to settle down, as it has wood resources and plenty of useful passive mobs.

BIOMES

Cherry Grove, Frozen Peaks, Grove, Jagged Peaks, Meadow, Snowy Slopes, Stony Peaks, Windswept Forest, Windswept Hills, Windswept Gravelly Hills

CAVE BIOMES

Cave biomes may not be super numerous in variations, but they are incredibly vast. Perfect for exploration, they challenge the player to ensure they're well-prepared for a casual spot of spelunking, with the off-chance of falling into an unexpected ancient city or lava pit. Players with a sense of adventure (or desire for treasure) will have to contend with some of Minecraft's most monstrous mobs down here.

BIOMES

Deep Dark, Dripstone Caves, Lush Caves

FLATLAND BIOMES

Flatlands are easily identifiable by being, well, flat. This means less trees than the usual biome and generally long, uninterrupted sight lines. These biomes can be grouped into two categories:

Plains: These flat and grassy biomes are great for setting up a home base. You'll be able to scout out caves and resources due to the easy sight lines, and you'll also likely be close by to another village or settlement.
Snowy Plains: These are a little less welcoming than their non-snowy counterparts. Rabbits and polar bears are native to these parts, along with strays and skeletons.

BIOMES

Plains, Sunflower Plains, Snowy Plains, Ice Spikes

HIGHLAND BIOMES

Highlands are biomes that exist way up on the Y-axis. The terrain is typically rugged, and you'll be no stranger to snow-covered peaks if you spend your time crossing them. These biomes can be divided into two groups:

Mountains: Mountains are made of peaks and slopes. While peaks are difficult to traverse, slopes (such as cherry groves) are more forgiving.

Windswept Hills: These biomes have very distinct features like floating rocks and islands, large waterfalls and overhangs. These biomes are more aesthetically pleasing than they are practical for survival - any water up here has to be covered or it will freeze.

BIOMES

Cherry Grove, Frozen Peaks, Grove, Jagged Peaks, Meadow, Snowy Slopes, Stony Peaks, Windswept Forest, Windswept Hills, Windswept Gravelly Hills

WETLAND BIOMES

Wet by both name and nature, wetlands range in enjoyability from sunny beach shores and picturesque rivers to muddy swamps and frozen rocks. This biome type is split into three categories:

Beaches: Life's a beach, with sandy shores and sea views. The only passive mobs that spawn here are turtles.

Rivers: Rivers in Minecraft have no currents, but they do generally lead to the ocean. While they can be quite calming for a little riverside fishing, they're the home to hostile drowned when the sun sets.

Swamps: Swamps are covered in foliage, with a lot of mud and pools of green water. The player might come across a rare swamp hut in this biome.

BIOMES

River, Frozen River, Swamp, Mangrove Swamp, Beach, Snowy Beach, Stony Shore

THE WILD

The Wild was one of the game's big major updates that landed back in summer of 2022. While the name might have been 'wild', it might have been better suited to 'The Creepy' - this is the update where things got real dark and spooky. Like Minecraft with the lights out.

WILD BIOMES

It's always fun when an update brings new biomes to the Overworld to explore, and the Wild brought us two - each as oddly dark and suspiciously damp as each other.

Deep Dark: This subterranean biome introduces itself pretty well with just its name. The cave biome is one of the most treacherous to navigate through - while it may house some of the rarest treasures in its ancient cities, it is also heavily guarded by the warden.

Mangrove Swamp: This biome can be found above ground, and is a variety of the pre-existing swamp biome. You can find it near warmer regions like deserts and jungles, and it's easily identifiable by its dense population of mangrove trees.

Looking for enchanted golden apples? Chests in an ancient city have the highest chance of containing them compared to chests in any other location.

WILD MOBS

These new environments needed new denizens, so the update also came with some new mobs to play with (or avoid for the sake of your life... you know, either or.). The allay, frog and tadpole were all new friendly mobs added. The warden was the only hostile, but it made up for being the only one by having enough hostility for all of them.

Want to know more about the mobs from this update? Check out the mobs chapter Minecraft Mobs on p. 28-31!

To promote The Wild, Minecraft released an online text-based adventure game called 'Craft Your Own Adventure: Wild Tales'! Check it out at

WILD RESOURCES

New biomes and beasts generally come with new resources for us to play with, and this update brought us sculk, mangrove wood and mud blocks to add to our collection, as well as other decorative must-haves for any swamp lovers like froglights.

TRICKY TRIALS

Welp! She's a big one! Tricky Trials is the newest expansion to drop in the world of Minecraft, and like other tentpole updates such as Caves & Cliffs and The Wild before it, things haven't quite been the same since she arrived.

TRIAL CHAMBERS

The main feature of this update is in the name itself. Minecraft is full of places to traverse and challenges to take on, but it's usually destroying a malevolent behemoth dragon or weighing up whether you'd rather slurp down rotten flesh or take the starvation death - these aren't real trials, though. Oh, no, sweet child.

Trial chambers are mysterious copper structures found underground, and serve as a mid-game combat challenge for players. Of course, the player is rewarded for all of their hard work with some well-earned loot post-trial, courtesy of trial spawners and vaults.

TRICKY MOBS

Breezes are new hostile mobs that are spawned by trial spawners. These bad boys are super agile and use wind as their weapon.

The update also brought us the bogged, a bunch of cute little rotting, poisonous skeletons that can be found in trials and in your regular old muddy swamp. Just another reason to keep milk handy, right?

NEW RESOURCES

Of course, new structures mean new resources. If you feel like constructing your own trial chamber (or just mimicking the casual deathtrap vibe in your humble abode), you're in luck - now you can play with copper and tuff blocks.

NEW WEAPONRY

It's been a while since we got a new weapon type, so Tricky Trials bringing us the mace is a pretty big deal! Maces are melee weapons that deal more damage the further a player falls before landing the blow. To craft one, you'll need to find components from (you guessed it) trial chambers: a heavy core (from ominous vaults) and a breeze rod (dropped from breeze mobs).

Here's a little tip - don't bother trying to create any distance between you and a Breeze for combat. They repel all projectiles, so long-distance warfare won't cut it.

SOUNDS OMINOUS...

As it should! And if you want it to sound even more ominous, why not go very literal? The ominous trial feature covers trial chambers and village raids. These are a great deal tougher than regular trials and raids, but they provide greater loot in return for your opt-in peril.

If you want to give an ominous trial or raid a go, then get your hands on an ominous bottle and slurp it down to gain the Bad Omen effect.

THE NEXT
BIG UPDATE

With Tricky Trials in place, it looks like it will be a while until the next big game changer update comes to Minecraft. In the meantime, why not make one yourself? Follow the prompts and design your own update for the game using the templates!

NEW BLOCKS

First things first - some new blocks! Let's create some new resources to build with in your new update. Be sure to think about designs etc. if it's a decorative block.

NEW MOBS

Every new update comes with new mobs to fight, so let's get to it!

A NEW HOSTILE ENEMY

A NEW TYPE OF VILLAGER

NEW BIOME

The best part of any update is exploring new environments! What's your environment like?

NEW SKINS

No disrespect to Steve and Alex, but sometimes we just want someone new to explore a new update with!

MINECRAFT MOBS

You're never alone in the world of Minecraft. All three dimensions are full of life, with mobs - short for 'mobile entity' - that are both friends and foes.

PASSIVE MOBS

These mobs are more than happy to coexist with you - some are happy to even join you on your adventures. Passive mobs won't attack you even if you attack them first.

Mob	Info
Allay	Can seek out items for you.
Axolotl	Can follow you into battle underwater.
Bat	N/A
Camel	Can be used as a mount (up to 2 players).
Cat	Can ward off phantoms and creepers.
Chicken	Drops feathers and raw chicken.
Cod	Drops raw cod and bonemeal.
Cow	Drops leather and raw beef.
Donkey	Can be used as a mount (with inventory).

Mob	Info
Fox	Bred foxes will defend you against mobs.
Frog	Drops froglights after eating magma cubes.
Glow squid	Drops glow ink sacs.
Horse	Can be used as a mount (with inventory).
Mooshroom	Drops leather and raw beef.
Mule	Can be used as a mount (with inventory).
Ocelot	Can ward off phantoms and creepers.
Parrot	Can detect hostile mobs within 20 blocks.

Mob	Info
Pig	Drops pork chops.
Pufferfish	Drops bonemeal.
Rabbit	Drops rabbit hide, raw rabbit and rabbit's foot.
Salmon	Drops raw salmon.
Sheep	Drops wool and mutton.
Skeleton horse	The fastest mount in game, and can be tamed if their rider is killed.
Sniffer	Can only be hatched from a sniffer egg. Sniffs out seeds from the ground.

Mob	Info
Snow golem	Can also be spawned by an enderman.
Squid	Drops ink sacs.
Strider	Drops string. Can be a mount.
Tadpole	Grow into frogs.
Tropical fish	Drops tropical fish and bonemeal.
Turtle	Drops sea grass.
Villager	Useful for trading and other services.
Wandering trader	Drops milk bucket.

NEUTRAL MOBS

Neutral mobs are happy to leave you to your business... unless provoked. If you pick a fight, they'll defend themselves and fight back.

Mob	Info
Bee	Can be farmed to collect honey and honeycomb.
Cave spider	Drops string and spider eyes.
Dolphin	Drops raw cod.
Drowned	Copper ingot, Trident
Enderman	Drops ender pearls.
Goat	Drops goat horns.
Iron golem	Killing a village Iron Golem lowers the player's village popularity by 10.
Llama	Can be used as a mount (with inventory).
Panda	Drops bamboo.
Piglin	Drops whatever it is holding.
Polar bear	Drops raw cod and raw salmon.
Spider	Drops string and spider eyes.
Trader llama	Can be used as a mount (with inventory).
Wolf	Can be tamed and helps the player in battle.
Zombified piglin	Drops gold nuggets and gold ingots.

HOSTILE MOBS

When it comes to hostile mobs, it's on sight! You better be ready to defend yourself when it comes to hostile mobs – they will attack you as soon as you step into their detection range (which ranges from 16 blocks all the way to 100 blocks).

Mob	Drop
Blaze	Blaze rod
Bogged	Bones, Arrows, Arrows of poison, Damaged bow
Breeze	Breeze Rod
Chicken jockey	N/A
Creeper	Gunpowder
Drowned	Copper ingot, Trident
Elder guardian	Prismarine shard, Wet sponge, Raw cod
Endermite	N/A
Evoker	Totem of undying, Emerald, Ominous banner
Ghast	Ghast tear, Gunpowder
Guardian	Raw cod, Prismarine crystal
Hoglin	Raw pork chop, Leather
Husk	Iron ingot
Magma cube	Magma cream
Phantom	Phantom membrane
Piglin brute	Golden axe
Pillager	Crossbow, Ominous banner

Mob	Drop
Ravager	Saddle
Shulker	Shulker shell
Silverfish	N/A
Skeleton	Bone, arrow
Skeleton horseman	N/A
Slime	Slimeball
Spider jockey	N/A
Stray	Bone, Arrow, Arrow of slowness
Vex	N/A
Vindicator	Emerald, Ominous banner, Iron axe
Warden	Sculk catalyst
Witch	Glass bottle, Glowstone dust, Gunpowder, Redstone, Spider eye, Sugar
Wither skeleton	Bone, Coal, Wither skeleton skull, Sword
Zoglin	N/A
Zombie	Iron ingot
Zombie villager	Iron ingot

You don't want to be caught unprepared when it comes to hostile mobs. Check out the Combat chapter (p. 52–53)

BOSS MOBS

Boss mobs are the most hostile of hostile mobs. They're supposed to pose as a challenge for the player, so they have a lot of health, a lot of strength and a lot of hostility.

■ **Withers** can be summoned by the player to take on. When a wither takes damage, it breaks all blocks within a 3x4x3 radius (and is thus the only mob able to destroy Obsidian). If defeated, a wither drops a nether star and 50XP.

■ The **ender dragon** can be found in its domain, the End. It is the ultimate challenge that Minecraft has to offer, as it has a ton of HP and is immune to all status effects. If you manage to defeat her (yes, her) then you'll get a dragon egg and 12,000 XP.

KNOW YOUR BLOCKS

The most basic unit of any Minecraft world is a block. The simple, humble block. The very foundation of every aspect of each of the vast and varied three dimensions and each of their vast and varied environments.

There are around 200 different kinds of blocks in this game, so here's a little list (okay, maybe not so little) of some of the more useful or common blocks you may come across on your adventures.

NATURAL BLOCKS

These blocks can be found spawning in nature, and can be harvested and then crafted. Natural blocks can be found in both the Overworld and the Nether, and can largely be grouped into five sub-categories.

GROUND	Note
Dirt	The basic block for farming. It's also a very accessible building block.
Mycelium	The dirt alternative found in mushroom island biomes.
Sand	Smelt to make glass, or mix with gunpowder to craft TNT.

PLANTS	Note
Cactus	Beware these blocks, as they hurt anything that comes into contact with it. They can only grow in sand.
Grass	A great farmland block when tilled with a hoe.
Log	The most versatile block. Logs can be crafted into planks and sticks to create the basis of many different items.
Melon, Pumpkin etc.	Sure, they make a great food resource, but they also have other uses. Wearing a pumpkin helmet prevents endermen from attacking you.

LIQUIDS	Note
Lava	While it's dangerous to acquire, it can be used to create stone and obsidian.
Water	The block of life, if you will. An absolute must have for farming, and always good to have in a bucket to deal with an unexpected fire.

STONE	Note
Bedrock	The indestructible block that is the foundation of the world.
Gravel	This can be used to suffocate unsuspecting mobs.
Obsidian	This block can only be damaged by the wither boss mob, so it's great for defensive builds. It is also required to create a nether portal.
Sandstone	A firmer form of sand that is great for building.

ORES AND MINERALS	Note
Coal Ore	A common ore useful for items like torches.
Copper Ore	Copper is the only block that changes its appearance over time. To prevent discoloration, wax copper blocks with honeycomb.
Diamond Ore	A rarer ore that is great for tools and armour.
Gold Ore	A rare ore that drops gold if mined with an iron pickaxe or higher.
Iron Ore	A common ore that is a good choice for early-game pickaxes.
Lapis Lazuli Ore	A rare ore needed to fuel enchantment. It can also be used for dyes and decoration.
Redstone Ore	An ore that drops redstone, a valuable resource for mechanical creations.

For more information on where to find ores (coordinate specific), check out p. 18–19.

STRUCTURAL BLOCKS

These blocks can be found, but they are usually part of generated structures. These are great to take and use to build your own place or structure.

Block	Note
Cobblestone	An excellent base construction material. It has mossy and deepslate decorative variations.
Concrete	Created when concrete powder and water mix, it can also be found dyed in trail ruins.
Stone Brick	A block found in stronghold structures. It has a mossy decorative variation.
Purpur	A purple block found in end cities and end ships.
Terracotta	A structural block found in badland biomes and deserts villages.

NETHER BLOCKS

Certain blocks are exclusive to the Nether dimension. They're harder to acquire, but definitely worth the trouble as they are some of the top resources available.

Block	Note
Glowstone	A light-emitting block that emits the highest light level in the game.
Nether Brick	A strong building material.
Netherrack	A great resource for bonfires.
Soul Sand	A block with many uses. Defensively, it can be used to slow the movement of anyone on it. It can also be used to plant nether wart, and to summon the wither mob.

DECORATIVE BLOCKS

Sometimes blocks just have to be cute #justgirlythings. There are tons of decorative blocks that are great for decorating your home.

Block	Use
Froglight	A light-emitting block made from a frog eating a magma cube.
Glass	Made by melting sand in a furnace. Using dye can tint the glass.
Wool	Obtained from sheep, this block can be dyed.

SCULK BLOCKS

This unique set of blocks are exclusively found in the deep dark biome. Sculk blocks drop experience when broken (except sculk vein, but no one cares about sculk vein anyway).

Block	Note
Sculk	Drops 1 experience.
Sculk Catalyst	Drops 5 experience. It converts surrounding blocks into sculk blocks.
Sculk Sensor	Drops 5 experience. It detects vibrations and triggers sculk shriekers.
Sculk Shrieker	Drops 5 experience. Summons a warden mob if triggered.

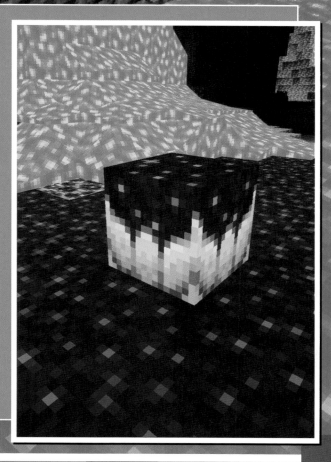

WHAT'S COOKING?

YOUR CHEF KIT

Everyone knows a chef is only as good as their tools, and since Minecraft mimics reality, it's no different in-game! If you want to master the michelin art of Minecraft, you'll need to kit yourself out with the following:

- Crafting Table (wooden plank x3)
- Furnace (cobblestone x8)
- Fishing Rod (sticks x3, string x2)
- Boat (wooden plank x5)
- Bowl (wooden plank x3)
- Bone Meal (bone x1)

Cooking makes use of the Crafting system - check out p. 46 for a more in-depth look at Crafting.

...n a rush for some ...oked meat? Get the ...op or steak straight ...om the source and ...t down the cooking ...process by killing ...mobs with fire.

Sometimes desperate times call for desperate measures! If you're dying of hunger and need to eat some rotten flesh (hey, we've all been there), then drink some milk right after - it'll cancel out the poison effect.

MINECRAFT MEATS

Meats are a great resource and one of the best (and most efficient) foods in the game to bring up your hunger bar.

Mob	Meat	Hunger Points (Raw)	Hunger Points (Cooked)
Cow	Beef	+3	+8
Mooshroom			
Pig	Pork	+3	+8
Chicken	Chicken	+2 (30% chance of food poisoning)	+6
Sheep	Mutton	+2	+6
Rabbit	Rabbit	+3	+5
Zombie	Rotten Flesh	+4 (80% chance of food poisoning)	N/A

FRESH FISH

You probably noticed the fishing rod and the boat up in the cooking kit - they're about to come to use! Kicking back in a rowboat with your rod can be a lovely way to chill and pass the time, but you can also find a bunch of fresh fish to chow down on.

Fish	Hunger Points (Raw)	Hunger Points (Cooked)
Fish	+2	+5
Salmon	+2	+6
Clownfish	+2	N/A

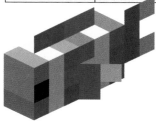
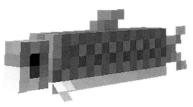

The vast variety of biomes means there is a vast variety of fruit and vegetables too. Produce is the food that keeps on giving, too - if you plant the seeds, you can start harvesting your own.

MINECRAFT MASTER CHEF

Sometimes it's about eating to thrive, not just to survive - right? Sure, hunger points are important, but there's nothing wrong with wanting to spice up things in the kitchen and getting a little Michelin up on the craft table. Here are some more enticing recipes to try:

GOLDEN APPLE

Gold Ingots x8, Apple x1

RABBIT STEW

Cooked Rabbit x1, Baked Potato x1, Carrot x1, Red/Brown Mushroom x1, Bowl x1

BIRTHDAY CAKE

Wheat x3, Egg x1, Milk Bucket x3, Sugar x2

HONEY BOTTLE

Glass Bottle x4, Honey Block x1

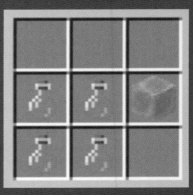

GOLDEN CARROT

Gold Nugget x8, Carrot x1

COOKIE

Wheat x2, Cocoa Beans x1

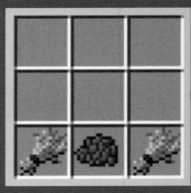

MUSHROOM STEW

Red Mushroom x1, Brown Mushroom x1, Bowl x1

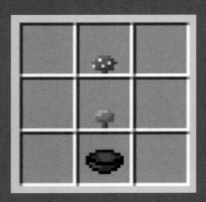

THE NETHERSEARCH

There's nothing like a good forage in a lava-filled hellscape, right? Can you find all of these things in the Nethersearch below?

T	E	M	M	Q	S	G	H	A	S	T	N	M	T	E	I	D
C	L	X	A	Z	S	S	T	R	H	N	E	F	H	N	B	G
K	X	A	H	G	K	A	O	X	R	I	T	O	G	D	W	Z
L	C	P	S	L	M	F	N	E	L	L	H	R	I	E	C	F
I	P	N	I	A	N	A	W	D	L	G	E	T	L	R	A	W
S	G	T	E	R	B	S	C	V	Z	I	R	R	M	M	T	B
S	A	L	X	B	N	A	B	U	M	P	R	E	O	E	K	A
O	J	P	O	I	U	L	J	N	B	W	A	S	O	N	I	N
F	S	J	L	W	A	C	Y	R	E	E	C	S	R	E	V	K
R	U	G	V	Z	S	L	V	R	P	Z	K	T	H	D	D	S
E	O	S	E	G	I	T	I	I	A	N	R	M	S	O	U	L
H	F	L	B	U	T	F	O	R	E	D	I	R	T	S	H	W
T	X	C	M	U	L	U	E	N	O	T	S	K	C	A	L	B
E	X	D	D	U	R	U	I	N	E	D	P	O	R	T	A	L
N	O	L	O	T	S	E	R	O	F	N	O	S	M	I	R	C
M	O	S	S	E	D	G	F	P	T	P	K	H	W	V	L	W
G	H	V	F	K	D	D	J	R	D	X	Y	A	E	Z	N	F

Hoglin	Strider	Magma Cube	Gold
Ghast	Basalt	Fortress	Endermen
Glowstone	Piglin	Blaze	Crimson Forest
Netherrack	Soul Fire	Blackstone	Nether Fossil
Nylium	Ruined Portal	Shroomlight	

NO PLACE LIKE HOME

There's nothing like returning to a safe place after a long day's adventuring. While exploring may be first on a lot of players' Minecraft agendas, it can be just as fun staying put and settling down – whether your dream home is a beachside property, a shack on top of a snowy peak or even a palace inspired by the architecture of ancient Greece, it's only a few blocks (well, a lot of blocks, if we're going for grecian palace) away...

HOME BENEFITS

Homes are a must-have for any adventurer, even if it's only in its most rudimentary form. Homes provide sanctuary from hostile mobs, and also serve as a great space to house your ever-expanding inventory. You can also invest in some light farm work to ensure you have your own supply of resources ready to go.

Looking for inspiration? Check out some of the free maps available in the Minecraft Marketplace to see what kind of architectural wonders you can build with blocks!

Pets are a great addition to any home! Ocelots and cats are perfect for keeping you company while also keeping creepers at bay.

Want to try a little community living? Move into an existing village or settlement! There's usually an empty home in these communities, and if not, you can always just steal a villager's (don't worry, we won't tell).

FINDING THE PERFECT SPOT

To be honest, there's no real answer to 'the best place to build a home'. There's definitely a good few wrong answers (don't even bother building one in the Nether - beds explode down there), but there's a lot of leeway when it comes to being correct. Aesthetically, it's really the player's choice; no one biome has 100% of the resources needed for the ultimate home, so it's all about what you're willing to settle down in, and how far you're willing to travel to source the things your chosen spot doesn't have.

So what should you consider when looking for a patch of land to lay down roots? Here's a little checklist for any prospective property developer:

▪ **Within a fair proximity to essential sources such as wood, food and ore.**
▪ **Near fertile soil if you want to consider farming.**
▪ **Close to water to enable fast travel via boat.**
▪ **Ideally with a little altitude to enable high ground advantage for any unwanted visitors.**

HOUSE BUILDING ESSENTIALS

Your vibe is your vibe. If you want to do your whole home out in all gold, go ahead; don't let anyone tell you how to decorate your home! But you might want to listen if someone tells you how to build your home, especially since there are some absolute essentials you don't want to miss:

▪ **Build your walls with some kind of stone-like block - basically anything that isn't flammable.**
▪ **Add doors and windows to keep your place secure from unwanted visitors but still full of light.**
▪ **Don't forget to add lights! Light sources keep away some of the hostile mobs in the game, so it's always a good idea to set torches (or some other light source) around your home and land.**
▪ **The first furniture you need to build is a bed - it's your new spawn point. From there, prioritise setting up chests, a crafting table and then some sort of food source.**

SPOT THE DIFFERENCE

There are eight differences to find between these two pictures - can you spot them all? Check out p. 62-63 for answers!

FRIENDLY MOBSEARCH

Not all mobs want to take you down - some are definitely worth seeking out to find and hang out with! Can you find the friendly mobs in the wordsearch below? Check out p. 62-63 for answers.

Z	G	P	X	L	K	B	O	S	S	L	E	S	G	E	D
F	E	W	M	T	F	K	C	L	E	H	Q	A	E	B	S
R	A	Z	Q	O	U	W	A	M	L	U	E	L	H	T	N
X	M	S	M	L	I	Q	A	V	I	I	T	E	I	P	I
U	O	A	O	O	O	C	X	D	M	R	D	B	P	D	F
R	C	L	T	X	T	J	P	C	U	D	B	A	I	H	F
H	L	K	K	A	I	E	W	T	I	A	H	D	M	B	E
M	O	O	R	H	S	O	O	M	R	O	P	O	T	R	R
V	I	L	L	A	G	E	R	T	R	W	H	N	O	E	A
W	L	Y	A	L	L	A	C	S	O	T	F	K	R	L	K
J	Q	G	M	Y	W	L	E	H	D	L	X	E	R	O	F
J	J	Q	M	U	P	P	R	O	I	C	E	Y	A	P	S
Q	B	C	A	T	Q	P	G	N	I	C	C	C	P	D	V
W	H	S	A	L	M	O	N	F	W	H	K	Z	O	A	N
R	E	D	I	R	T	S	X	D	M	E	B	E	D	T	U
W	Q	Z	Q	T	E	E	Q	W	K	I	Z	M	N	U	H

Allay	**Chicken**	**Parrot**	**Squid**
Armadillo	**Donkey**	**Rabbit**	**Strider**
Axolotl	**Horse**	**Salmon**	**Tadpole**
Camel	**Mooshroom**	**Sheep**	**Turtle**
Cat	**Ocelot**	**Sniffer**	**Villager**

INVENTORY ESSENTIALS

You might be quick to name your pickaxe or your diamond sword as your most useful weapon, but it's actually something a lot more unassuming (and not equippable, either): your inventory.

Your inventory comes with you wherever you go, so you better take good care of it! Sure, you can get away with a free-for-all kind of vibe in the first few days, but the best survival runs are those that get real serious about managing your inventory to maximum efficiency.

Minecraft is all about resources, so it's best to keep on top of your items – if you find yourself ambushed by an unexpected horde of creepers, or falling deeper into caves than you intended, then you want to make sure you're equipped with the right items to get you out of a pinch, instead of say... a plethora of potatoes.

HOME STORAGE

Of course, this is Minecraft, so you're going to be coming across an abundance of items - way more than 27. That's where storage comes in - anything you don't need to hand should be going in a chest in your home base.

If you're serious about hunkering down, why not build a room dedicated to only chests? That means everything's in one place, and you'll always know where to find things instead of running around your home and checking all the nooks and crannies. You'll want to categorise your storage, too - one for armour, one for food, one for tools etc.

YOUR INVENTORY

There are 27 slots available in your inventory, which seems like a lot... and it does at the beginning, sure, but you'll find later in-game, you'll be wishing you had more. It's best to split your 27 slots down into these categories:

■ **Weapons – 2 slots:** You need one and a back-up, and it's always good to have different types for a little bit of variety. Oh, and don't forget to stack them up for spares.

■ **Tools – 2 slots:** You only really need one type of pickaxe, but you may require another if you come across a bit more of a niche mineral on your adventure.

■ **Lighting – 1 slot:** Stack up some torches for a good supply of emergency lighting.

■ **Food – 1 slot:** Stack up on a cooked meat of your choice to keep your hunger bar topped up.

■ **Crafting Utilities – 4 slots:** You might need to create things on the go, so be sure you're carrying the likes of crafting tables and furnaces instead of having to scramble and make them from scratch.

■ **Utility Items – 6 slots:** This is more general and open to interpretation, but it's always a good idea to carry the likes of a ladder, bucket, compass etc,

■ **Potions – 4 slots:** Okay, so this is more for the late game play, where you'll need some potions to make your traversal a little easier. The likes of Fire Res and Night Vision are always useful for caving.

■ **Dealer's Choice – 7 slots:** The last slots are totally up to you. It's probably a good idea to keep them open - you never know what you'll find out there and want to take back with you.

BAGGAGE ALLOWANCE

If you've decided you want to move base to a new location, or you're going for say... a little extended trip, why not consider going by boat? Boats are super useful, as they can carry a chest, which means you can transport a lot of items with you.

MASTER YOUR CRAFT

Crafting is a key part of the Minecraft experience - it's in the name, after all. Whether you're looking to make something to hang on your wall, or something to take on pig demons in another dimension, it's all to be made at the humble craft table.

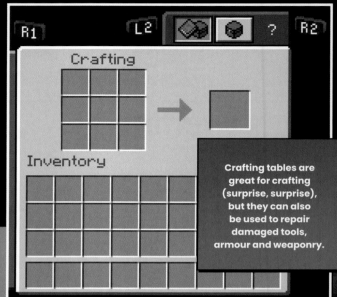

Crafting tables are great for crafting (surprise, surprise), but they can also be used to repair damaged tools, armour and weaponry.

CRAFTING GRID

Crafting is a grid-based process, with players having a very basic 2x2 grid in their inventory. This simple grid allows very elementary recipes to be made on the go, but the majority of recipes require a 3x3 grid. 3x3 grids are available using a crafting table.

CRAFTING RECIPES

If you're wondering how to make something, your Recipe Book holds all of the possible crafting recipes (alongside other recipes for smelting and brewing).

Recipes can be unlocked via gameplay, whether it's finding a new material or even just stepping foot in a new biome for the first time.

Whoever said "patience is a virtue" has clearly never needed to know how to make glazed terracotta ASAP. If you need to know a recipe before you discover it in the wild, check out some of the online catalogs with crafting grids (like www.minecraft-crafting.net).

CRAFTING QUIZ

The best crafters out there have their recipes down to muscle memory. How well do you know your craft? Identify the ingredient combos below, and check out p. 62-63 to see if you got them right.

1

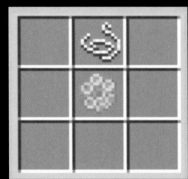

2

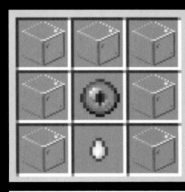

3

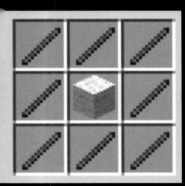

4

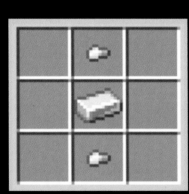

5

6

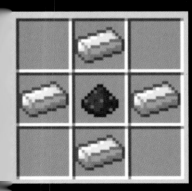

7

8

9

HOW ENCHANTING

Enchanting is a system that comes into its own mid-to-late gameplay. At this point, you've worn your crafting table to the bone, and you've made some really great pieces. Now what? Well, why not try making those pieces a little more advanced? A little more magical, perhaps?

The enchanting process allows you to augment your existing equipment with powerful buffs, but unlike crafting and smelting, it's not a guaranteed outcome. If you try to enchant something, you risk the whole thing failing and taking the original item along with it. Ready for a little risk?

Practice really does make perfect! The higher your experience level, the better your enchantments will turn out. Enchantment success chances are also boosted by your enchantment set-up. Putting your enchantment table near bookshelves grants a little enchantment boost - you can place up to 15 to get the maximum buff.

LET'S GET ENCHANTING

To start enchanting, we'll need an enchanting table, which can be made on our trusty old crafting table. Enchanting tables require four obsidians, two diamonds and one book.

But a mere enchanting table isn't enough - each enchantment will require lapis lazuli and XP for fuel.

KNOW YOUR ENCHANTMENTS

There are about thirty types of enchantments available, and each type has its own different rankings. Compared to processes as straightforward as crafting, enchantment can be a little intimidating to work out, and the lapis lazuli requirement makes it quite costly to experiment and try things out. To save you time, energy, ores and XP, here are the best enchantments (and their ranks) you should be prioritising:

■ **Mending (I):** Mending is always worth its cost, as wear and tear strikes at even the highest-end pieces of gear. This enchantment gives XP

bubbles the ability to repair, which means using your weapons also has the chance to heal them.

■ **Efficiency (I–V):** Minecraft is all about resource gathering, so making that process easier is a no-brainer. Enhancing tools with Efficiency increases your mining speed. You may also want to consider Fortune (I) to increase the amount of drops.

■ **Sharpness (I–V):** Enchantments that augment your weapon power are always a good idea, but unlike some of the more weapon-type-specific enchantments (like Channelling or Piercing), Sharpness covers and enhances most weaponry. Power (I–V) is another broad stroke augment to consider.

■ **Protection (I–IV):** As stated above, the broader stroke augments are better choices to opt for before getting too niche. Protection lessens damage taken from a broad range of sources.

■ **Feather Falling (I–IV):** Enchanting your boots with Feather Falling reduces fall damage, which is a great augment to have while climbing cliff sides or exploring caves.

It's possible (rare, but possible) to get your hands on some pre-enchanted items in the wild, without needing any lapis lazuli or XP. There's a chance to find enchanted items via lucky drops from powerful mobs, looting from the End City, or trading emeralds with piglins or villagers.

BIOMES CROSSWORD

All seasoned adventurers pay attention to their surroundings. Can you solve these clues and identify the biomes? Check out p. 62–63 for answers.

Across:

1. This biome has mineshafts and terracotta [8]
2. This biome was inspired by a painting by a Swedish artist [4, 5]
4. This red forest is found in the Nether [7, 6]
5. This is the rarest biome in Minecraft [8, 6]
7. This biome has vines and parrots [6]
9. A witch calls this biome home [5]
10. This biome has beautiful pink petalled trees [6, 5]
11. The panda calls this biome home [6, 6]

Down:

1. Trail Ruins usually spawn in this biome [5, 6]
3. These snowy plains are covered in glaciers [3, ●]
6. Sculk blocks are exclusive to this biome [4, 4]
8. This Nether biome is home to striders and endermen [6, 6]

MINECRAFT MAZE

Yikes! You were caving when your torch went out. Can you find your way out without bumping into any of the Wardens? Check out p. 62–63 for the solution.

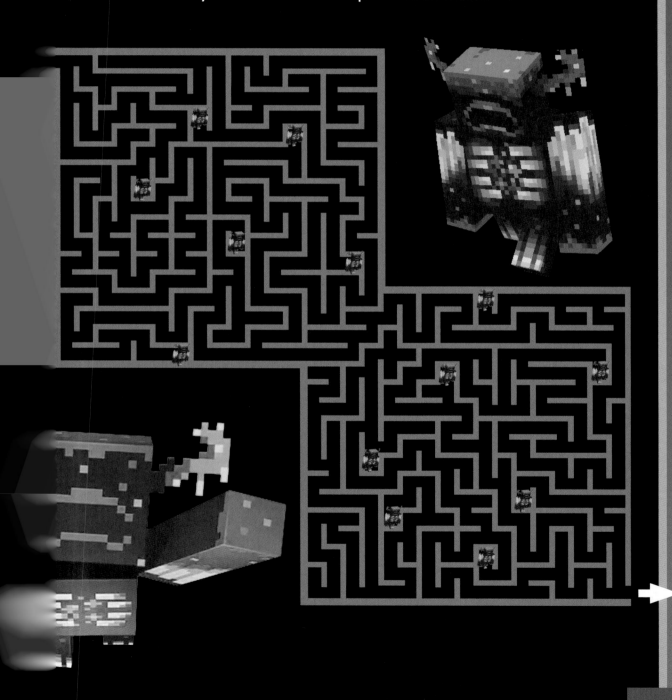

THE PRINCIPLES OF COMBAT

Survival is the name of the game in Minecraft, and while a big part of that is finding resources to sustain you, another part is warding off the entities that are actively trying to have you meet your end. Whether you're just trying to survive your unexpected encounters or going after some of the game's ultimate bosses, you need to know the basics of combat.

Timing is key to all encounters. Try timing your attack just before the enemy is about to strike you - interrupting an enemy attack gives you time to reposition before striking again.

WEAPONS

Minecraft has six types of weapons: swords, axes (which are technically classed as tools), tridents, bows, crossbows and the newest addition, the mace.

Close Range Combat

Weapons: Swords, Axes, Tridents, Maces

Close-range combat is frantic, but a cool head and practised method will always see you coming out on top. Try to find higher ground (even just a one block advantage will do it) so you have the chance to land a crit with a jump attack.

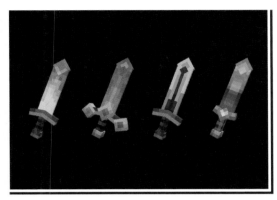

Long Range Combat

Weapons: Bows, Crossbows

Sometimes a more strategic approach is to take the battle at a distance. Bows and crossbows work similarly in that the shot distance, power and damage depend on how hard you pull the weapon back. Minecraft uses real-world flight physics, so arrows lose force the further they have to travel before striking their target.

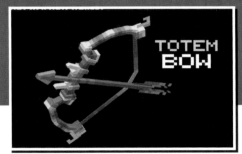

Listen up! Make sure your audio settings are optimised for you to catch any mobs trying to sneak up on you. Player and mob footsteps are classified as separate sounds in Minecraft, so quietening player footsteps mean you'll always be able to identify incoming footsteps as potential threats.

SHIELDS

Shields are optional additions to your gear set-up, but they're definitely worth consideration. Blocking hits can protect against incoming damage, and they can also absorb explosions. Use six wooden planks and one iron ingot to craft a shield (you can also add a banner to make it patterned, if you're feeling fancy).

ARMOUR

Armour is a must-have for any Minecrafter, even for those trying to keep things passive (hey, you never know when you might get a surprise visit from an exploding creeper). The most basic armour set can be crafted with 24 iron ingots, but you can make stronger sets with rarer ores (you can also find some pretty snazzy sets from chests in villages).

Make use of friendly mobs in combat! Tamed wolves can make great travelling company and will have your back in any unexpected fights in the wild. Oh, and ocelots and cats are great for defending your home while you rest.

GUESS THE MOB

How keen is your eye when it comes to identifying mobs out in the wild? Use the mob behaviour hints below and see if you've got your mob mastery down! Check out p. 62–63 for answers.

1. **I can mimic the sound of nearby mobs.**

2. **I turn into a bowl if struck by lightning.**

3. **I guard villages and offer flowers to villagers.**

4. **Feed me raw cod to earn my trust.**

5. **I'll follow you if you're holding seeds.**

6. **Deflect my fireballs back at me for a free hit.**

7. **I'll teleport to avoid water.**

8. **If you catch me, I'd pass on eating me for dinner.**

9. **My favourite meals are magma cubes and slimes.**

10. **I'll guard your home and keep you safe if you tame me.**

TAKING COMMAND

Minecraft is a great game to customise, and nothing really makes a game your own more than using commands. These magical incantations allow you to summon sniffers, teleport to taigas, and even take command of the skies above! Here are some of the most useful commands for you to try out.

Command	Description
/teleport [target] <destination>	Teleport yourself (or a target) to a specific location via coordinates.
/weather <clear/rain/ thunder>	Change the weather.
/time set <time>	Set the time of day, either using numbers (ex. "1000" for 10am) or daytimes (ex. noon, night etc.).
/summon <entity> [x] [y] [z]	Sick of waiting for the 1% chance for something to spawn? Summon whatever you want to specific coordinates.
/kill [target]	Well… pretty self-explanatory, no?
/locate <category> <thing>	If you can't be bothered looking for a biome or structure, use this to get the nearest coordinates. Then you can use the /teleport command to take yourself there.
/gamemode <mode>	If you want to switch between game modes (like switching to Survival after finishing your Creative build), you can use this command to do so seamlessly.
/difficulty <difficulty>	Use this command to switch between game difficulties (i.e. peaceful, easy, normal, etc.).
/give <target> <item> <quantity>	Get any in-game item with this command.
/enchant <target> <enchantment> [level]	Sometimes enchantment can be a slog, so no one's going to judge you for skipping a few steps with a command or two. We won't tell!

BLOCK SCRAMBLE

Can you unscramble these Minecraft blocks? Don't worry, we've given you the first letter of each block as a hint! Check out p. 62-63 for answers.

1. CALY

2. MLEMIUCY

3. BSTALA

4. SOLU SNAD

5. BOCERDK

6. OABIINSD

7. TTARETRAOC

8. CTBEOSNEBOL

9. GOOELTNSW

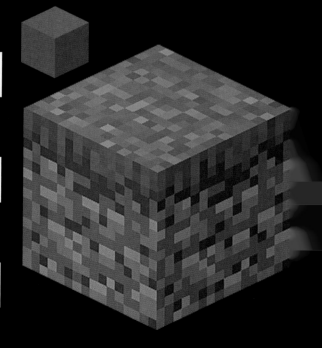

BREWING PUZZLE

Let's get to brewing some potions! Can you work out which glass potion will fill up with potion first? Check out p. 62-63 for the answer.

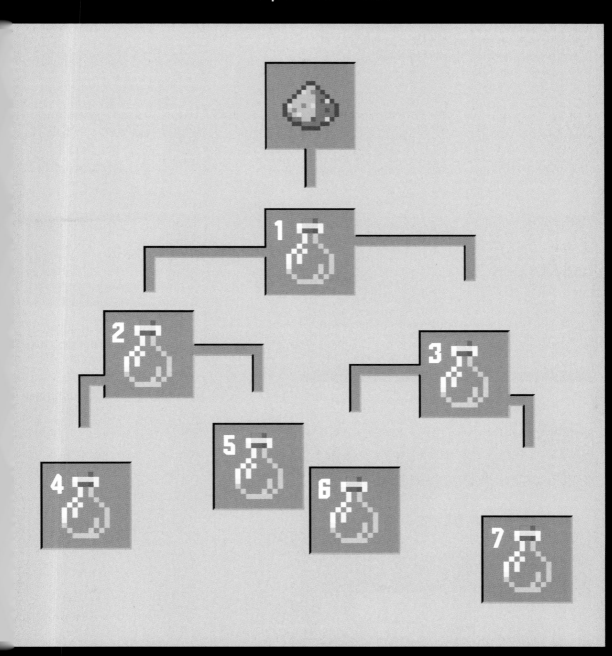

FIFTEEN YEARS OF MINECRAFT

2024 was a big year for Minecraft - it marked fifteen years in our favourite world of blocks! Minecraft celebrated with a free 15 Year Journey map courtesy of Oreville Studios. The map housed the Minecraft Museum, hallowed halls that hold tribute to some of the most iconic points in Minecraft's history.

Have you visited the Minecraft Museum yet? Download the map for free on the Minecraft Marketplace!

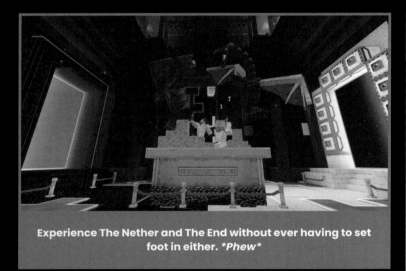

Experience The Nether and The End without ever having to set foot in either. *Phew*

Make your way through the museum finding stickers for your sticker book.

Learn about major updates like Caves and Cliffs!

HAPPY BIRTHDAY, MINECRAFT!

Take a (literal) trip down memory lane and look back at some of Minecraft's proudest moments.

Play exhibition themed mini-games along the way.

RING RUSH!

Grab your Elytra and soar through the End Dimension. Complete three laps to set the fastest time!

PLAY   CLOSE

Visit cool exhibitions to learn more about different aspects of Minecraft!

THE END QUIZ

So you've made it to The End... of this guide! We might not have an enderdragon waiting for you, but we do have our very own final boss: this mega quiz! See whether you truly can call yourself a Minecraft Maestro and take on The End Quiz – check out p. 62-63 for answers!

1. **What does a creeper drop when it's killed?**

2. **What tool do you need to crop farms?**

3. **What element are endermen afraid of?**

4. **What do you need if you want to tame a parrot?**

5. **What is the weakest sword in the game?**

6. **Which biome is home to pandas?**

7. **What drops if you trick a skeleton into shooting a creeper?**

8. **What item will lead you to a stronghold?**

9. **Which dimension are you most likely to find gold in?**

10. **What does a frog need to eat to create froglights?**

11. **Which enchantment lessens fall damage?**

12. What mineral ore is required to work an enchantment table?

13. What mob can you ride across lava in the Nether?

14. What armour type will make piglins passive?

15. Which ore can be used to create machines?

16. What mob do wandering traders travel with?

17. What item does the Wither drop when defeated?

18. What was the first enemy added to Minecraft?

19. What can you wear to prevent triggering an enderman's attack?

20. What is the one block that shows age over time?

21. What does a villager turn into when struck by lightning?

22. Which biome is home to foxes?

23. Which ore is most likely to spawn at extreme heights?

24. What is the one block you cannot jump on?

25. What potion helps you see in the dark?

ANSWERS

J-21: FIND STEVE AND ALEX

39: THE NETHERSEARCH

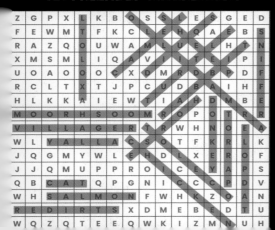

42: SPOT THE DIFFERENCE

43: FRIENDLY MOBSEARCH

47: CRAFTING QUIZ

1. Bed
2. Candle
3. End Crystal
4. Painting
5. Chain
6. Gold Helmet
7. Compass
8. Boat
9. Shulker Box